49 Easy English Conversation Dialogues For Beginners in American English:

Vocabulary for TOEFL, TOEIC and IELTS

Jackie Bolen

www.eslspeaking.org

2

Table of Contents

4

About the Author: Jackie Bolen

I taught English in South Korea for 10 years to every level and type of student. I've taught every age from kindergarten kids to adults. Most of my time has centered around teaching at two universities: five years at a science and engineering school in Cheonan, and four years at a major university in Busan where I taught upper-level classes for students majoring in English. In my spare time, you can usually find me outside surfing, biking, hiking, or snowshoeing. I now live in Vancouver, Canada.

In case you were wondering what my academic qualifications are, I hold a Master of Arts in Psychology. During my time in Korea, I completed both the Cambridge CELTA and DELTA certification programs. With the combination of almost ten years teaching ESL/EFL learners of all ages and levels, and the more formal teaching qualifications I've obtained, I have a solid foundation on which to offer advice to English learners.

I truly hope that you find this book useful. I would love it if you sent me an email with any questions or feedback that you might have.

Jackie Bolen (www.jackiebolen.com)

Twitter: @bolen_jackie

Email: jb.business.online@gmail.com

You might also be interested in this book: Advanced English Conversation Dialogues. It has hundreds of helpful English idioms and expressions. You can find it wherever you like to buy books. Learn to speak more fluently in American English.

Introduction

Welcome to this book designed to help you expand your knowledge of American English. My goal is to help you speak and write more fluently.

Let's face it, English can be difficult to master, even for the best students. In this book, you'll find American English dialogues that are ideal for beginners.

The best way to learn new vocabulary is in context.

To get the most bang for your buck, be sure to do the following:

– Review frequently.

– Try to use some of the phrases and expressions in real life.

– Don't be nervous about making mistakes. That's how you'll get better at English!

– Consider studying with a friend so you can help each other stay motivated.

– Use a notebook and write down new words, idioms, expressions, etc. that you run across. Review frequently so that they stay fresh in your mind.

– Be sure to answer the questions at the end of each dialogue. I recommend trying to do this from memory. No peeking!

– I recommend doing one dialogue a day. This will be more beneficial than finishing the entire book in a week or two.

Good luck and I wish you well on your journey to becoming more proficient with American English.

The Four-Step Reading Process

Here's what I recommend doing for each of the dialogues in order to get the most benefit from them.

#1: Read the Introduction

Be sure to read the introduction at the start of each dialogue. This helps to set the context and will make what you're reading more memorable. Think about if you've experienced a similar situation before.

#2: Read the Conversation Quickly

Read the whole conversation through quickly, without stopping to look up words or phrases. If you don't know something, make your best guess as to what it is. Think about the overall meaning and what's happening.

#3: Read for Detail

Go back and read the conversation one more time. Look up words that you don't know and write them down in a notebook. If you don't understand everything, read the dialogue again.

#4: Read the Questions and Answer Them

There are three questions at the end of each dialogue. Read them carefully and see if you can answer them from memory. If you can't, go back and find the answer in the dialogue. Check your answers.

Meeting Someone New

Tim and Zeke are meeting for the first time at Sam's party.

Tim: Hi, I don't think I know you. My name is Tim.

Zeke: Nice to meet you. My name is Zeke.

Tim: So how do you know Sam?

Zeke: Well, we were **co-workers years ago** at ABC **construction company**. How about you?

Tim: Oh, I'm Sam's neighbor. I live **next door** to him.

Zeke: I see. It's a nice **neighborhood**. When did you move here?

Tim: **Years ago**. It's changed a lot but in a good way.

Zeke: Well, nice to meet you. I'm going to **grab** another drink.

Vocabulary

Co-workers: People that work together.

Years ago: Many years in the past.

Construction company: A company that builds buildings.

Next door: The house beside.

Neighborhood: An area where people live.

Grab: Get.

Practice

1. Just wait. I want to _____ my jacket before we go.

2. Cindy and I were _____ until quite recently.

3. Which _____ are you thinking about moving to?

4. I met Tony _____. We played soccer together.

5. You should move _____ to me! I would be so happy.

6. I've heard bad things about that _____. Be careful.

Answers

1. grab

2. co-workers

3. neighborhood

4. years ago

5. next door

6. construction company

The Coffee Shop Recommendation

Keith and Sara are discussing coffee shops near their office.

Keith: I need a coffee and I'm so tired of the stuff here at work. It's terrible.

Sara: You're **100% right** about that. I usually go to Monk's Coffee. It's just around the corner.

Keith: Oh. I've never been there. Why do you like it?

Sara: They **roast** and **grind** their own **coffee beans**. It makes a big difference.

Keith: Okay. I'll **head over there** now. Do I turn right or left when I **exit** the building?

Sara: Turn right and walk **one block**. You'll see it on your left.

Keith: Thanks so much! I'm excited to try it.

Vocabulary

100% right: Totally correct.

Roast: Heat or cook something in an oven.

Grind: Make smaller by using force.

Coffee beans: The part of the coffee plant that becomes coffee, after roasting and grinding.

Head over there: Go to a certain place.

Exit: Leave.

One block: An area of land in a city. Usually a square or rectangle.

Practice

1. It's not far. Just walk _____ and look to your right.

2. I'm going to _____ a ham for Easter dinner.

3. I prefer Arabica _____ to other kinds.

4. Can we _____ that agreement without any penalties?

5. I'm not arguing. I know that you're _____.

6. If you _____ your own beans before you make coffee, the results are much better.

7. We're going to be late. Let's _____ right now.

Answers

1. one block

2. roast

3. coffee beans

4. exit

5. 100% right

6. grind

7. head over there

Sorry I'm Late

Linda is apologizing to Carrie for being late for their dinner meeting.

Linda: Carrie, I'm so sorry I'm late. I feel terrible.

Carrie: It's no problem. I ordered a beer and caught up on my **social media**. What happened?

Linda: There was a big **traffic jam**. There must have been a **car accident**.

Carrie: Oh, too bad. I hate it when that happens.

Linda: Did you look at the **menu** yet? What are you having?

Carrie: I can't decide. Maybe the pizza but I do love spaghetti with meatballs as well.

Linda: Hmm...a tough decision for sure. Let me have a look and figure out what I want.

Carrie: If you also can't decide, we can maybe **split** two **dishes**?

Linda: Sure, let me look and see.

Vocabulary

Social media: Facebook, Pinterest, Twitter, etc.

Traffic jam: Moving slowly, or not at all when driving due to many cars on the road or an accident.

Car accident: When a car hits an object, another car, person, etc.

Menu: The list of what you can order at a restaurant.

Split: Share.

Dishes: A plate or bowl of food at a restaurant. Example: Spaghetti with tomato sauce is one dish. Thai salad with chicken is another dish.

Practice

1. How many _____ should we order for 6 people?

2. I got into a _____ last week.

3. Should we _____ the bill?

4. Let's leave early. There's always a _____ at this time.

5. Can I see the _____, please?

6. Facebook is my favourite _____.

Answers

1. dishes

2. car accident

3. split

4. traffic jam

5. menu

6. social media

Long Time, No See

Tom runs into Nancy at the shopping mall after not seeing her for a long time.

Tom: Nancy! Hi. **Long time, no see**.

Nancy: It has been **a while**.

Tom: Wasn't it last **holiday season**? I think I was doing some **last-minute** shopping.

Nancy: I'm sure you're right. It must have been. I'm famous for shopping on **Christmas Eve**. What's up with you?

Tom: Same old, same old. Busy at work. Doing stuff with the kids. The usual. How about you?

Nancy: Oh, I got a new job at ABC Law. It's going well.

Tom: Congratulations!

Vocabulary

Long time, no see: An expression you can say to someone if you haven't seen them in a few months or a year.

A while: Not a short time period.

Holiday season: Generally refers to November and December in North America, Europe and other places around the world.

Last-minute: At the last possible time.

Christmas Eve: The evening of December 24th.

Same old, same old: An expression to say that nothing has changed since the last time talking.

Practice

1. Hey Ted! What's up? Oh, _____.

2. Judy! _____. Why haven't you been at soccer lately?

3. Things are so different this _____ because of Covid-19.

4. My family loves watching Home Alone on _____.

5. It's going to be _____ before dinner. If you're hungry, why don't you have a snack?

6. I have to do some _____ things for work. Can I call you in about an hour?

Answers

1. same old, same old

2. long time, no see

3. holiday season

4. Christmas Eve

5. a while

6. last-minute

Hold the Mayo

Tim's order is wrong at a restaurant.

Tim: Excuse me, I ordered my burger with no mayo. But, I think there's some on it. I hate mayo.

Waitress: The kitchen must have missed that. I had that on the order. Can I get you a new one?

Tim: Yes, please.

Waitress: No problem. It should be about 10 minutes.

Tim: Thank you.

Waitress: Sorry for getting that wrong.

Check your Understanding

1. What does Tim not like?

2. Did the waitress make a mistake?

3. How long will it take to make a new burger?

Answers

1. He doesn't like Mayo.

2. No, the people cooking the burger did.

3. It will take about 10 minutes.

At a Fast Food Restaurant

Sara is ordering food at a fast food restaurant

Employee: Hi, what can I get you?

Sara: I'd like a double cheeseburger meal, please.

Employee: Sure, **what kind of drink** would you like?

Sara: Do you have Pepsi?

Employee: No, just Coke.

Sara: Okay, I'll have that.

Employee: Anything else?

Sara: Oh, no mustard on that burger, please. And also no onions.

Employee: Okay.

Sara: That's everything.

Employee: Is that **to stay** or to go?

Sara: Hmm....what time is it? 12:15? To stay is fine. Thank you.

Vocabulary

What kind of drink? : At a fast food restaurant, this usually means what kind of soda.

To stay: Eating inside the restaurant.

Check your Understanding

1. What kind of drink does Sara get?

2. What does Sara order?

3. What does Sara not want on her burger?

4. Why does she decide to eat in the restaurant?

Answers

1. She gets a Coke.

2. She orders a double cheeseburger meal.

3. She doesn't want onions or mustard.

4. She decides to eat in the restaurant because she has enough time.

Which Bus Can I Take?

Todd is trying to take the bus downtown.

Todd: Excuse me, do you know where I can **catch the bus**?

Man: Depends where you're trying to go. There are **a few** bus stops around here.

Todd: Oh, I want to go **downtown**.

Man: Okay. Well, you should cross the street and walk two **blocks** towards Granville. You'll see it there.

Todd: Okay. Thank you. Do you know the bus number I can take?

Man: I'm not sure but I think maybe the 10 and the 12. I think it says on the sign what the **final destination** is.

Todd: Okay, I'll have a look then. Thanks so much for your help. I really appreciate it.

Man: No problem.

Vocabulary

catch the bus: Get on the bus.

a few: 3-5 of something.

downtown: The center of a city, usually with tall office buildings.

blocks: A certain area in a city, usually a square or rectangle.

final destination: Last stop.

Practice

1. What's your _____?
2. There are _____ Korean restaurants around here but I think Insadong is the best one.
3. Walk four _____ and you'll see it on your left. You can't miss it.
4. You can _____ to the airport across the street from here.
5. I hate going to _____ Vancouver on weekdays. Traffic is so bad.

Answers

1. final destination
2. a few
3. blocks
4. catch the bus
5. downtown

I'd Like to Make an Appointment

Tom is making an appointment with his doctor on the phone.

Tom: Can I make an appointment for tomorrow, please?

Jenny: Sure, with which doctor?

Tom: Dr. Brown.

Jenny: We have nothing tomorrow but how about Wednesday?

Tom: Sure, that's fine.

Jenny: Okay, I'll put you in for 2:00?

Tom: Sounds good.

Jenny: What are you coming in for?

Tom: I have a sore toe.

Jenny: Okay, we'll see you on Wednesday.

Check your Understanding

1. Why does Tom want to see his doctor?

2. When is he going to see the doctor?

3. What is his preferred appointment day?

Answers

1. He wants to see his doctor because he has a sore toe.

2. He will see his doctor on Wednesday at 2:00.

3. His preferred appointment day is tomorrow.

Making a Reservation

Lucy is making a reservation for her wife's birthday party.

Waitress: Hi, Luciano's. How can I help you?

Lucy: I'd like to make a **reservation** for July 8th at 6:00, please.

Waitress: Okay. For how many people?

Lucy: I'm not **100% sure** yet. I think between 8 and 10 people.

Waitress: Okay. We'll save a table for 10 people then. Is it a **special occasion**?

Lucy: Yes, it's my wife's birthday.

Waitress: Will you bring a cake or would you like us to make one?

Lucy: Oh...umm...I'll bring my own I think.

Waitress: Do you prefer inside or on our **covered patio**?

Lucy: Oh, patio for sure. That sounds **fantastic**.

Waitress: Okay. What's your phone number?

Lucy: It's 123-456-7890.

Vocabulary

Reservation: Saving something for a certain date and time. In this case, a table for 10 people.

100% sure: Certain.

Special occasion: For example, birthday, anniversary, graduation, wedding, etc. Not normal days.

Covered patio: An eating or hanging out area that is protected if it's raining.

Fantastic: Really good.

Practice

1. It's supposed to be rainy this weekend. Hmm...why don't we go to the Cactus Club? They have a big _____.

2. Is it a _____ tonight?

3. I have a _____ for Tuesday at 3:00 that I'd like to cancel, please.

4. You're pregnant? That's _____ news!

5. I'm not _____ yet if I can come, or not. Can I let you know in a few days?

Answers

1. covered patio

2. special occasion

3. reservation

4. fantastic

5. 100% sure

Going to the Beach

Tanya and Shannon are talking about going to the beach the next day.

Tanya: Shannon, I checked the **weather forecast. Highs** of 28 tomorrow and sunny. Let's go to the beach.

Shannon: Really? Yeah, let's go!

Tanya: Should we go to Jericho Beach?

Shannon: Yeah, that's a nice place. There's not a lot of **parking** though. Should we go later at like 4:00 when all the families have left?

Tanya: Definitely. We can stay for the **sunset.**

Shannon: **Rad.** Why don't I **pick you up** around 3:30?

Tanya: Awesome. I'll see you then.

Vocabulary

Weather forecast: Prediction for the weather in the coming days. Temperature, rainy, cloudy, etc.

Highs: The highest possible temperature in a day.

Parking: A place to put a car when you're not driving it.

Sunset: When the sun is going down in the evening.

Rad: Great; awesome.

Pick you up: Come get you.

Practice

1. I'll _____ at 3:00. Is that okay for you?

2. What's the _____ like there? Maybe expensive? Should we take the subway instead?

3. That's so _____ about your new boyfriend! He's so cute.

4. The _____ is showing rain all weekend. Maybe we should cancel our camping trip.

5. I love to catch the _____ at the beach whenever possible.

6. There are _____ of only 7 overnight. Be sure to dress warmly.

Answers

1. pick you up

2. parking

3. rad

4. weather forecast

5. sunset

6. highs

Where do you Live?

Toby and Casey are co-workers who are talking about where they live.

Toby: Traffic was so bad this morning!

Casey: Oh, I don't have a **commute**. I just walk to work. Where do you live?

Toby: I live in Edgemont.

Casey: Wow, that's far! How long does it take you to get to work?

Toby: Well, **optimistically**, only 30 minutes. But, it's usually closer to an hour. Where do you live?

Casey: You know the **high rise** across the street? That's where I live.

Toby: Amazing. I'd go home for lunch if I was so close.

Casey: I often do. I guess people think I **go out for lunch** but I'm usually just **hanging out** at home.

Vocabulary

Traffic: Cars on a road.

Commute: Travelling between home and work.

Optimistically: Describing the best possible situation or outcome.

High rise: A building that is at least 10 floors.

Go out for lunch: Eating at a restaurant for lunch.

Hanging out: Spending time in a relaxed way.

Practice

1. Ted and I are _____ on Sunday but I'm not sure what we're going to do yet.

2. I hate having a long _____. That's why I'm thinking about moving.

3. _____, I think that I can do both things tomorrow.

4. Do you want to _____ on Thursday?

5. _____ was so bad today. That's why I'm late.

6. There are both pros and cons to living in a _____.

Answers

1. hanging out

2. commute

3. optimistically

4. go out for lunch

5. traffic

6. high rise

The New Car

Sam is talking to his friend Ed about his new car.

Sam: Ed! Whose **wheels** are those? So **flashy**.

Ed: They're mine! I bought a new car last week.

Sam: Really? Awesome! It looks **super sharp**. Can we go out for **a ride**?

Ed: Yeah, sure. Why don't we **cruise** down to the beach?

Sam: Okay. Let's go. Let me grab my wallet and phone.

Ed: Sure.

Vocabulary

Wheels: A car.

Flashy: Exciting; shiny; new.

Super: Very; really.

Sharp: Describes something that looks good.

A ride: A trip in a car.

Cruise: Driving casually, without worrying too much about time or the final destination.

Practice

1. Do you want to go for a _____ later? Maybe we could go to the beach?

2. I'm not sure if I have _____, or not. Let me ask my mom.

3. I'm _____ hungry right now. Can we stop and pick something up?

4. Do you need _____ to the airport?

5. Wow! That's a _____, new haircut that you have. Who cut it for you?

6. Tony, you look _____ today. Is that a new suit?

Answers

1. cruise

2. wheels

3. super

4. a ride

5. flashy

6. sharp

Out Walking the Dog

Trina sees her neighbor Bob when walking her dog.

Trina: Hey Bob! How are you?

Bob: Pretty good. I don't remember you having a dog. Did you just get him?

Trina: It's a girl. Yeah, we got Riley last week.

Bob: Nice. Where did you get her?

Trina: At the shelter. I let the kids pick her out. She was super friendly and it was an easy choice.

Bob: And how's it going at your house?

Trina: Well, Riley ruined our couch and has eaten a ton of shoes already but I don't care. She's so funny and cute. I love her so much already.

Bob: Sounds like exciting times at your place.

Check your Understanding

1. Who is Riley?
2. Where did Trina get Riley?
3. What are the positives and negatives about Riley?
4. When did Trina get Riley?

Answers

1. Riley is Trina's dog.
2. She got her at the animal shelter (a place for animals without homes)
3. Riley is funny cute, and friendly. However, she likes to eat things like the couch or shoes.
4. She got her last week.

Asking for Money

Steve is asking his Dad for some money.

Steve: Dad, I need twenty **bucks**.

Dad: Didn't I just give you your **allowance?** What happened to that?

Steve: My friends and I went out for lunch yesterday at school. It's all gone.

Dad: So what do you need the **cash** for?

Steve: Everyone is going out for lunch today too.

Dad: You can bring lunch from home and it's **free**! Seriously. Just take anything you want out of the fridge. No charge.

Steve: So will you give me the money?

Dad: No. I don't **eat out** as much as you do and I'm the one who makes all the money!

Steve: Daaaaaaadddd! It's so **unfair.**

Dad: Have you thought about getting a **part-time job**?

Vocabulary

bucks: Dollars.

allowance: Spending money that parents give their children weekly or monthly.

cash: Money.

free: Describes something that doesn't cost any money.

eat out: Buying food outside the home.

unfair: Not fair; unreasonable.

part-time job: A job that is less than 40 hours per week.

Practice

1. I just got a new _____ at that restaurant down the street.

2. No charge. These samples are _____.

3. Mom! It's so _____ that you won't let me take the car this weekend.

4. I give my kids $10 a week for _____.

5. Do you have any _____ on you? I think that food truck doesn't take credit cards.

6. I _____ way too much. It's why I don't have any money!

7. Seriously? That bottle of water costs seven _____? I'd rather be thirsty.

Answers

1. part-time job

2. free

3. unfair

4. allowance

5. cash

6. eat out

7. bucks

What's on TV?

Jerry and Linda are talking about what they're watching on Netflix.

Jerry: What are you watching on Netflix these days?

Lana: The Crown. It's so good. Have you seen it?

Jerry: I know everyone is talking about it but I'm just not interested in the Royal family.

Lana: So what are you watching?

Jerry: Well, I love sports stuff so I've been watching Drive to Survive.

Lana: Oh, what's that?

Jerry: It's about the Formula One racing teams. It follows them from race to race and you see the behind-the-scenes stuff. I don't like racing but it's pretty addictive. I binged an entire season in one weekend.

Lana: I'll have to check that out.

Check your Understanding

1. What is Lana watching on TV?
2. What's Jerry watching?
3. How long does it take Jerry to watch one season of Drive to Survive?
4. What kind of things does Jerry like to watch on TV?

Answers

1. She's watching The Crown about the Royal family.
2. He's watching Drive to Survive about Formula One racing.
3. He watched it in one weekend.
4. He likes watching sports things.

Moving

Amy is asking Zeke for help with moving.

Amy: Hey Zeke, you have a **truck**, right? Can you help me **move next weekend**? I think it'll take about three hours. Is $100 **fair**?

Zeke: I do have a truck and I can also help you move.

Amy: Great! I appreciate it.

Zeke: But, I don't want your money. That's what friends are for, right?

Amy: Zeke! I know everyone probably wants you to help them because you have a truck, right? It must get annoying.

Zeke: You are the first person I've helped this year. It's **all good.**

Amy: Okay. Well, we'll get some pizza and beer afterwards. **My treat.**

Zeke: That sounds great.

Vocabulary

Truck: A type of vehicle that has a box at the back.

Move: Change houses.

Next weekend: The following Saturday and Sunday.

Fair: Reasonable; appropriate.

All good: No problem.

My treat: I'll pay.

Practice

1. Why don't we go out for dinner? It's _____.

2. I think I'm going to buy a _____. I need it for my new business.

3. What do you think is a _____ punishment for that?

4. Hey, it's _____. Don't even worry about that.

5. What are you doing _____? Why don't we catch a movie?

6. I have to _____. My landlord sold this place.

Answers

1. my treat

2. truck

3. fair

4. all good

5. next weekend

6. move

A Slow Laptop

Min-Gyu is talking to Kiyo about her slow laptop.

Min-Gyu: Let's watch a movie.

Kiyo: Sure, I'll fire it up on my laptop. We can find one on Netflix.

Min-Gyu: Sounds good.

Kiyo: Okay...hmmm...it takes a long time to turn on.

Min-Gyu: Wow. Is this normal?

Kiyo: It usually takes 2-3 minutes.

Min-Gyu: Mine turns on in about 10 seconds. How old is your laptop?

Kiyo: I don't know. Maybe eight years?

Min-Gyu: What??? That's so old for a computer. That's why it's so slow. You should get a new one.

Kiyo: Oh, this one is fine.

Min-Gyu: Really? It still hasn't even turned on yet!

Check your Understanding

1. What is the problem?
2. What do Kiyo and Min-Gyu want to do?
3. Why is the computer very slow?
4. What is Min-Gyu's advice?

Answers

1. Kiyo has a very old computer that takes a long time to turn on.
2. They want to watch a movie on Netflix.
3. It's likely slow because it's so old.
4. His advice is to get a new computer.

Pizza for Dinner?

Ted is talking to his husband Tony about what to eat for dinner.

Ted: Tony, what should we have for dinner?

Tony: Hmm...what do we have in our fridge? Maybe we could have a tofu stir-fry? We have lots of vegetables we need to eat I think. I'll make that homemade sweet & sour sauce that you like.

Ted: That doesn't sound exciting to me. Why don't I pick up a pizza on the way home from work?

Tony: Ted! Didn't we agree to stop spending so much money on take-out? I'll make the stir-fry, you lazy guy!

Ted: Yes, we did agree to stop spending so much money. You can cook me dinner then. If you insist. But let's put pineapple in too. You know how much I love that.

Tony: I'll do it. It's only because I love you so much though.

Ted: I love you too.

Check your Understanding

1. Who wants to get a pizza and who wants to cook at home?
2. Why does Tony think they should cook at home?
3. What is Tony going to cook?

Answers

1. Ted wants to get pizza and Tony wants to cook at home.
2. He thinks they should cook at home because they spend so much money on take-out food.
3. He's going to make a sweet & sour stir-fry with tofu and vegetables.

Air Jordans

Tom is looking for some Air Jordans.

Tom: Excuse me, I'm looking for the Air Jordans in a size 8.5.

Clerk: Hmmm...let me check for you. Just a second. I'm not sure we have that size left. They're super popular.

Tom: Sure.

Clerk: Okay, I see that we should have a couple of pairs. Let me grab one for you to try on. What color were you interested in? We have black or white.

Tom: I'd love the black ones, please.

Clerk: Okay, I'll go get those. I'll be back in a minute.

Tom: Sure, thanks.

Check your Understanding

1. What color of shoes does Tom want?

2. Does the store have a lot of Air Jordans?

3. Does the store have the size that Tom needs?

Answers

1. He wants to get the black shoes.

2. No, they don't.

3. Yes, they do.

The New House

Liz is talking to Cheryl about her new house.

Liz: Didn't you just move? I think I heard you **mention** that.

Cheryl: Yes, I moved to Coquitlam from Maple Ridge.

Liz: Oh, exciting! Why did you move?

Cheryl: Well, I was tired of **commuting** so far. I work **downtown** and Coquitlam is around 20 minutes closer.

Liz: For sure. How's everything at the new place?

Cheryl: Well, it's smaller so I've had to **downsize**. But it's easier having fewer things. I'm starting to **embrace simplicity**.

Liz: I need more of that in my life! I feel like I'm always cleaning and looking after my things.

Cheryl: Check out that Netflix show with Marie Kondo. She was my **guide**. Everything you own should bring you joy.

Liz: I'll have a look. I need a new show to watch.

Vocabulary

Mention: Say; speak.

Commuting: Travelling between home and work.

Downtown: The center of a city, usually with tall office buildings.

Downsize: Give away or sell things that you own.

Embrace: Love.

Simplicity: In this case, means not having many things or possessions.

Guide: A person that you follow or seek advice from.

Practice

1. Let's hire a _____. I'm a bit nervous about doing this alone.

2. _____ is terrible. Why don't we move closer to work?

3. I need to _____ to get ready to move.

4. _____ is so much easier than having lots of stuff. I just borrow whatever I need.

5. Don't forget to _____ that you have a coupon before you order.

6. What's the best way to get _____? I think parking is too expensive there.

7. I want to _____ my brother's wife but she's just so annoying.

Answers

1. guide

2. commuting

3. downsize

4. simplicity

5. mention

6. downtown

7. embrace

I'd Like a Refund, Please

Tom would like to get his money back for a t-shirt he bought.

Tom: I'd like to exchange this t-shirt, please.

Clerk: Is there anything wrong with it?

Tom: Oh no, I bought it for my daughter but she doesn't like the color.

Clerk: Okay, I see. Do you have the receipt?

Tom: Yes, right here.

Clerk: Okay, would you like a refund or would you like to exchange it?

Tom: A refund is great.

Clerk: Do you have the credit card you bought it with?

Tom: Yes, I do.

Check your Understanding

1. Why is Tom returning the shirt?

2. How did Tom pay for the t-shirt?

3. Does Tom want his money back?

Answers

1. He is returning the shirt because his daughter didn't like the color.

2. He paid with a credit card.

3. Yes, he does.

Let's Clean the House

Sandy and Logan are talking about cleaning the house this weekend.

Sandy: So what are we going to do **this weekend**?

Logan: Our house. It's so **disorganized** and **filthy**. We need to clean it up.

Sandy: Really? I don't think it's that bad.

Logan: It's bad. Do you not see all those **fuzzy** things in the fridge?

Sandy: I have noticed that, yes. But you always **take care of** that.

Logan: Okay, I will. But what about all those dishes on the counter and the toilets that haven't been **scrubbed** in weeks?

Sandy: Okay, you're right. Let's do that Saturday morning.

Logan: Sure. Let's do a good job though. I want everything to **sparkle.**

Vocabulary

This weekend: The upcoming Saturday and Sunday.

Disorganized: Not organized or tidy.

Filthy: Very dirty.

Fuzzy: In this case, refers to food that is moldy or bad.

Take care of: Handle.

Scrubbed: Cleaned deeply.

Sparkle: Describes something that is extra clean.

Practice

1. I want this car to _____.

2. I hate being so _____. I don't know how to solve this problem though.

3. Those strawberries are _____. Don't eat them.

4. I _____ the bathtub but it's still not that clean. Do you have any advice?

5. I want to clean the garage _____.

6. My car is so _____. I just throw my trash on the seat next to me.

7. I want to _____ all the weeds in the garden tonight.

Answers

1. sparkle

2. disorganized

3. fuzzy

4. scrubbed

5. this weekend

6. filthy

7. take care of

Feed the Cat

Sammy's Mom is telling him to feed his cat.

Mom: Sammy, why are Fluffy's food and water bowls empty?

Sammy: Mom. You can just fill them. Why do you keep bugging me about this?

Mom: Do you remember before we got Fluffy that we talked about this? You agreed to be the one to feed her and make sure her bowls were always full. Do you remember that?

Sammy: MOM! Yes, I do.

Mom: Okay, so what's happening then?

Sammy: It's so annoying. I hate doing it. The cat food smells bad.

Mom: Well, how do you think Fluffy feels? She is hungry and has no food. Or is thirsty and has no water. How would you feel if you came to dinner and there was no food for you to eat

Sammy: I'd be sad and angry.

Mom: Well, that's how Fluffy feels.

Sammy: Okay, fine. I'll do it.

Mom: Okay, but I don't want to keep reminding you. You are not going to get your allowance if I have to remind you even once about it.

Check your Understanding

1. Who is Fluffy?
2. Why is Sammy's mom annoyed at him?
3. What will happen if Sammy forgets again?

Answers

1. Fluffy is the pet cat.
2. She is annoyed because Sammy forgets to fill up Fluffy's food and water bowls.
3. He will not get his allowance.

What's that Smell?

Monty's dad is wondering about a smell in his room.

Dad: Hey Monty. Are you almost ready to go? We're leaving in 10 minutes. Wait...what's that smell? It **stinks** in here.

Monty: Okay. I'll be ready. I don't know what that smell is.

Dad: It's not a normal smell. Do you have some **rotting** food in here?

Monty: I don't think so.

Dad: Let's take a look. I'm sure that's what it is.

Monty: DAD! It's nothing.

Dad: What's on your desk and under your bed? Hmmm...I think this is it! What was in this bowl? There's **mold** all over it.

Monty: I was eating ice cream **a few** nights ago.

Dad: Gross. Clean up after yourself. Put that in the **dishwasher** but **rinse it out** first.

Vocabulary

Rotting: Describe food that is going bad because it is old or not in the refrigerator.

Mold: What grows on food when it is old or bad.

A few: 3-5.

Dishwasher: A machine that washes dishes.

Rinse it out: To use water to clean something.

Practice

1. Your bowl has chunks of pasta sauce on it. Please _____ before you put it into the sink.
2. You can still eat cheese that has some _____ on it. Just cut it off.
3. Let's buy a _____. I'm so tired of washing dishes by hand.
4. I want to get _____ more shirts before I start this new job.
5. Please clean out all the _____ food from the fridge before I come back from grocery shopping.

Answers

1. rinse it out
2. mold
3. dishwasher
4. a few
5. rotting

Ordering Chinese Food

Ken and Lana are talking about getting Chinese food for dinner.

Ken: Let's get some Chinese food for dinner tonight.

Lana: Sure, what about the Wok Dragon? That place is so good and it's also cheap.

Ken: Yes, definitely. I like their sweet & sour chicken balls. The fried rice is good too.

Lana: Sure, and I want the broccoli and tofu stir-fry.

Ken: Do you want to call and I'll go pick it up?

Lana: Don't they deliver for free if you live within 3 kilometers?

Ken: Oh maybe.

Lana: I'll ask when I order.

Ken: Sure, that sounds good.

Check your Understanding

1. Why do they like the Wok Dragon?
2. What's Lana's favourite dish there?
3. Will they pick up the food or get it delivered?

Answers

1. They like it because it's both good and cheap.
2. She likes the broccoli and tofu stir-fry.
3. We don't know yet. Lana is going to ask if they have free delivery.

Put Away your Laundry

Cara's dad is telling her to put away her laundry.

Dad: Hey Cara. Your **laundry** is done. Come **put it away**.

Cara: Dad, I'll do it later.

Dad: No, you won't. It'll still be sitting here in a week from now.

Cara: I'm **busy** now.

Dad: It looks like you're playing **Candy Crush**. You don't seem busy at all.

Cara: I'll do it later.

Dad: Okay, well you have two choices here. The first one is that you do your own laundry from now on. You are 13 and old enough to **handle it** yourself. The second is that you come put it away now. It's **up to you**.

Cara: Fine. I'll put it away.

Dad: Thank you, my sweet loving daughter. And you're welcome for doing your laundry for you! I love how you appreciate me so much.

Vocabulary

Laundry: Refers to clothes that are either dirty or after they have been washed.

Put it away: To place something in the correct spot.

Busy: Doing something else.

Candy Crush: A cellphone game.

Handle it: Take care of.

Up to you: Your choice or decision.

Practice

1. I don't care where we eat. It's _____.

2. I have to do _____ tonight. I don't think I have anything to wear to work tomorrow.

3. Are you _____ this weekend? Let's go hiking.

4. I know that he's a difficult client but I think that you can _____.

5. Please look after your computer. _____ when you're done with it and don't just leave it on the couch.

6. I'm addicted to _____.

Answers

1. up to you

2. laundry

3. busy

4. handle it

5. put it away

6. Candy Crush

Eating Habits

Sara and Lucy are talking about bad eating habits.

Sara: Long time, no see. What's up?

Lucy: Oh, not much. Just watching way too much TV and eating junk food. All my activities got cancelled because of Covid.

Sara: Same here. I'm so bored. I just eat chips and popcorn and watch movies almost every night.

Lucy: I totally get that. You know what. We should start going for walks once or twice a week at night. What do you think?

Sara: That's the best idea. I need to get out of the house more and get some exercise.

Lucy: Okay, let's start tomorrow night. I'll come to your house around 7:30. Would that work?

Sara: Sure, sounds good.

Check your Understanding

1. Why are Sara and Lucy bored?
2. What are they going to do together?
3. When is their first walk?

Answers

1. They are bored because their activities got cancelled because of Covid-19.
2. They are going to go for walks at night together.
3. Their first walk is tomorrow at 7:30.

I'm so Tired

Terry is talking to Sandra about how tired he is.

Terry: I wish I hadn't stayed out so late last night. I feel **terrible** today.

Sandra: You also drank way too much beer. Do you have a **hangover**?

Terry: Probably, yeah. What's going on today? Anything?

Sandra: Nothing really. I was going to catch up on some work. Maybe go for a bike ride.

Terry: Okay. I think I'm going to take a nap then.

Sandra: Good plan. **Catch some Z's** and you'll feel better.

Terry: Wake me up in time for dinner, okay? I don't want to sleep **too long** because I won't be able to sleep tonight.

Sandra: Sure thing.

Vocabulary

Terrible: Really bad.

Hangover: Feeling sick because of drinking too much the day before.

Catch some Z's: Get some sleep.

Too long: Longer than is good or appropriate.

Sure thing: Definitely; okay.

Practice

1. You'll get into Harvard. It's a _____ I think.

2. Drink some water too if you don't want to have a _____.

3. It's been _____. Let's get lunch soon.

4. I have a _____ cold and can't come.

5. I need to _____ before we go out tonight.

Answers

1. sure thing

2. hangover

3. too long

4. terrible

5. catch some Z's

Driver's License

Tom is asking to renew his driver's license.

Clerk: Hi, how can I help you.

Tom: I need to **renew** my **driver's license**.

Clerk: Sure, do you have your card?

Tom: Yes, here it is.

Clerk: Oh. It **expired** more than two years ago. You haven't been driving lately?

Tom: No, I sold my car. But I'm moving and will need a car to get to work now.

Clerk: I see. Well, you can't renew a license that is more than two years old. You'll have to take the **driving test** and get a new one.

Tom: Really? You can't make an **exception**?

Clerk. No, **I'm afraid not**. Would you like to **schedule** a test now? You can also schedule it **online**.

Tom: I'll do it now.

Vocabulary

Renew: Extend the time period for something.

Driver's license: A document that allows someone to drive.

Expired: To be not valid because it is past the time allowed.

Driving test: A test that you need to pass before getting a driver's license.

Exception: An instance of not following a rule.

I'm afraid not: An expression that means, "Sorry, I can't."

Schedule: To book a certain time for something.

Online: Using the Internet.

Practice

1. You can take the test _____. It's easier than driving all the way to the test center.

2. I think this milk is _____. Does it smell sour?

3. I have to _____ my license.

4. I can't make an _____ for you. Sorry.

5. My son just got his _____. I'm so happy he can drive himself to work now!

6. Can I _____ an MRI for next month?

7. I failed my _____ on the first try too. It happens a lot.

8. Sorry, _____. You'll have to bring your ID next time.

Answers

1. online

2. expired

3. renew

4. exception

5. driver's license

6. schedule

7. driving test

8. I'm afraid not

Please Cancel my Appointment

Tom would like to cancel his dentist appointment.

Tom: Hi, I'd like to cancel my appointment, please.

Clerk: Sure, what's the name?

Tom: Tom Waits.

Clerk: When is your appointment?

Tom: It's at 9 am tomorrow.

Clerk: Oh, we have a $50 cancellation fee for less than 24 hours. Would you still like to cancel?

Tom: Yes, please. I'll pay the fee.

Clerk: Okay, I got it. Would you like to reschedule?

Tom: No, thanks. That's okay.

Clerk: Okay, take care.

Check your Understanding

1. Why does Tom have to pay $50?

2. Does he want to reschedule?

3. Why does he want to cancel his appointment?

Answers

1. He has to pay $50 for cancelling within 24 hours.

2. No, he doesn't.

3. We don't know why he wants to cancel it.

55

It's Hot in Here

Brenda and Ho-Hyun are talking about how hot it is in their house.

Brenda: This **heat wave** is crazy. It's **boiling** in here.

Ho-Hyun: For real. It must be at least 30 degrees in our bedroom.

Brenda: Why don't we get **air conditioning**? I know it's expensive but it'll be worth it.

Ho-Hyun: It'll be more than a thousand **bucks**. And we'd only use it for 4-5 days a year. It's not worth it.

Brenda: I know you're right. I'm just worried that we'll get **heatstroke** in our own house!

Ho-Hyun: You're not going to get heatstroke. Trust me. Why don't we go to the store and buy another fan? That way, we can each have one pointing at us at all times.

Brenda: Sure, and let's get some ice cream and **refreshing** drinks too.

Ho-Hyun: Okay, let's go. And how about going to the movie theater first and catching **a flick** It's always nice and cool in there.

Vocabulary

Heat wave: Several unusually hot days in a row.

Boiling: In this case, describes a very hot air temperature (commonly used to describe water that has reached 100 degrees).

Air conditioning: A machine that cools down the air inside a building.

Bucks: Dollars.

Heatstroke: An illness that is caused by too much time in a hot place, especially when exercising or in the sun.

Refreshing: Cool and nice.

A flick: A movie.

Practice

1. Do you want to catch _____ with me on Friday night?

2. Turn up the _____. It's so hot in here.

3. There's going to be a _____ next week.

4. Jump in the lake. It's very _____.

5. It's _____ in the car. Can you roll down the windows?

6. I got _____ when I went hiking in July.

7. I think it costs around ten _____.

Answers

1. a flick

2. air conditioning

3. heat wave

4. refreshing

5. boiling

6. heatstroke

7. bucks

Sushi for Dinner

Tim is ordering some sushi.

Tim: Hi, can I put in an order for 12:30, please?

Waiter: Sure, that's for pick-up?

Tim: Yes, please.

Waiter: What would you like?

Tim: 1 combo A and 1 vegetarian combo.

Waiter: Okay. Would you like miso soup with that?

Tim: Is it included?

Waiter: Yes.

Tim: Sure, I'll take two then.

Waiter: Okay, what's your name and phone number?

Tim: Tim. 778-385-2821.

Check your Understanding

1. Is Tim getting the sushi delivered?

2. What is Tim ordering?

3. Does he have to pay extra for the soup?

Answers

1. No, he's picking it up.

2. He's getting two combos and two miso soups.

3. No, he doesn't.

Save the Environment

Tammy is annoyed at Doug for not recycling.

Tammy: Doug, I took out the **trash** this morning and I saw all kinds of things that can be recycled.

Doug: Like what?

Tammy: Well, pickle **jars**, soda cans, **tin cans, flyers**. Almost everything in the trash could have been recycled.

Doug: Well, how do you know it was me?

Tammy: You're the only person who lives here besides me. And I always **recycle.** I care about the **environment.**

Doug: Are you saying that I don't care about it?

Tammy: Well...I think you could do more.

Doug: Hmmm. I don't know about that.

Vocabulary

Trash: Garbage.

Jars: Glass (usually) containers that something like pickles come in.

Tin cans: What canned food like corn or tomatoes come in.

Flyers: Paper advertisements that are delivered to houses.

Recycle: To use something again. For example, turning old tires into a running track.

Environment: The world as a whole.

Practice

1. My kids are amazing. They're always thinking of ways to save the _____.

2. Ted! Take out the _____. It's your chore this week.

3. I know that _____ can be recycled but I think it takes a lot of energy to do that.

4. Please _____ this instead of throwing it into the garbage.

5. Do you have any old _____? I'm making kimchi and need some.

6. How can we stop getting so many _____? I'm tired of them.

Answers

1. environment
2. trash
3. tin cans
4. recycle
5. jars
6. flyers

New Glasses

Kara is talking to Bev about her new glasses.

Kara: Bev, did you get new glasses? You look different.

Bev: Yeah, I did. Thanks for noticing! Do you like them?

Kara: They're funky. You look so young.

Bev: That was my goal. Plus, I can see better as well which is important too I guess.

Kara: Haha! Yes, the problem with getting old, right?

Bev: I know. It's tough times for sure.

Kara: Where did you get them? I need a new pair myself.

Bev: At ABC Optical. It's in New Town Center. They're having a big sale. Buy 1 pair, get 1 for free.

Check your Understanding

1. Why does Bev look different?
2. Does Kara like the new glasses?
3. Why does Bev recommend ABC Optical?

Answers

1. She looks different because she got new glasses.
2. Yes, she likes them.
3. She recommends them because they're having a buy 1, get 1 free sale.

Hey, Slow Down

Sam is driving too quickly.

Harry: Hey, slow down buddy! You're driving way too quickly.

Sam: Nah, it's fine. Just relax.

Harry: Seriously. I feel so scared. Please slow down.

Sam: Stop worrying so much. This is how I drive all the time.

Harry: Please pull over. I want to get out.

Sam: How are you going to get home?

Harry: I'll take the bus.

Sam: Okay, okay. I'll drive like a grandma.

Check your Understanding

1. How is Harry feeling? Why?

2. Why does Harry want Sam to pull over?

3. Does Sam agree to slow down?

Answers

1. He's feeling scared because Sam is driving too fast.

2. He wants him to pull over so he can get out.

3. Yes, he agrees to drive more slowly (like a grandma!)

Do you Want to Leave a Message?

Tom wants to talk to Jim.

Tom: Hi, could I please talk to Jim?

Receptionist: Jim Ford?

Tom: Yes, please.

Receptionist: Okay, I'll put you through.

Tom: Thank you.

Receptionist: He's not answering. Would you like to leave a message?

Tom: Oh. Do you know when he'll be back?

Receptionist: He's probably on lunch right now. You could try again in an hour?

Tom: Sounds good. I'll do that.

Check your Understanding

1. Is Jim in the office now?

2. Does Tom want to leave a message?

3. Does the receptionist know where Jim is?

Answers

1. No, he's not.

2. No, he'll try calling back later.

3. He guesses that Jim is on lunch but he's not sure.

Pet Peeves

Bo-Hyun and Amir are talking about their pet peeves.

Bo-Hyun: So do you have any **pet peeves**?

Amir: So many. Where to start. My biggest one is **slow walkers**. And then getting **stuck** behind them on a **sidewalk**. What's one of yours?

Bo-Hyun: Oh yeah, that's annoying for sure. Hmm...I hate TV commercials. So much. That's why I only watch Netflix these days. Or, I'll pay for **live streaming** for sports.

Amir: I know, right? Who wants to sit through that?

Bo-Hyun: Every time I see an **ad** for ice cream or fast food, I want to go out and buy it! It's not easy to **resist**.

Amir: I feel your pain, my friend.

Vocabulary

Pet peeves: Things that annoy someone.

Slow walkers: People who walk extra slow.

Stuck: Trapped.

Sidewalk: A raised area next to a road where people can walk.

Live streaming: Watching something as it happens through the Internet.

Ad: Advertisement.

Resist: Not give in to something or someone.

I feel your pain: An expression that means, "I understand your situation."

Practice

1. _____. Break-ups are so difficult.
2. Let's pass these _____.
3. Is there _____ for the French Open? I don't have cable TV.
4. Watch out for that big crack on the _____.
5. One of my _____ is people who are late.
6. I have some delicious ice cream in my freezer and I'm trying to _____ eating all of it in one day!
7. Did you see that new _____ for Air Jordans?
8. I'm _____ at my job even though I don't like it because unemployment is so high.

Answers

1. I feel your pain
2. slow walkers
3. live streaming
4. sidewalk
5. pet peeves
6. resist
7. ad
8. stuck

Board Games

Cayla and Jill are talking about playing some board games.

Cayla: You like board games, right?

Jill: Yeah, most games. Just not Cards Against Humanity. I hate that one.

Cayla: Me too. Don't worry. Do you want to come play some games this weekend? I have two other friends coming over and we're looking for a fourth person.

Jill: Definitely. When are you playing?

Cayla: Saturday afternoon at 1:00.

Jill: Awesome. I'll be there for sure. Text me your address.

Cayla: Sure. I'll do it later.

Jill: I'll bring some of my homemade wine too.

Cayla: Awesome.

Check your Understanding

1. What do Jill and Cayla think about Cards Against Humanity?
2. How many people are going to play card games?
3. Does Jill know Cayla's address?

Answers

1. Neither of them likes that game.
2. Four people are going to play games.
3. No, she doesn't. Cayla will text it to her.

Ordering a Coffee

Carrie is ordering a coffee from a barista.

Barista: Hi, what can I get for you?

Carrie: I'll have an iced vanilla blend, please. Does the vanilla one have a shot of coffee in it?

Barista: No, it doesn't. But we can add a shot of espresso if you'd like.

Carrie: Sure, that sounds good.

Barista: What size would you like?

Carrie: I'll have a medium.

Barista: Okay, anything else?

Carrie: I am a bit hungry. I'll have one of your Italian paninis as well.

Barista: Okay. Is this to stay or to go.

Carrie: To stay, please.

Check your Understanding

1. What does Carrie order?
2. Where is she eating?
3. Does she want some coffee in her drink?

Answers

1. She orders a medium iced vanilla blend with a shot of espresso and an Italian panini.
2. She's going to eat in the coffee shop.
3. Yes, she does.

Shopping for Clothes

Andrew is asking the clerk for a different size.

Clerk: Can I help you with anything?

Andrew: Yes, I hope so. I like this shirt but there's only small and medium. I need a large.

Clerk: Oh, let me look. Hmm...I don't see any. Do you want me to check online for you?

Andrew: Sure.

Clerk: Okay, there are lots of larges. Do you want to order it online? Or, I can get it delivered to this store for pick-up tomorrow.

Andrew: Oh, I think I'll order it myself and get it delivered to my house.

Clerk: Sounds great. Do you need anything else today?

Andrew: No, I think that's it. Thanks for your help.

Check your Understanding

1. What does Andrew want?

2. Why is Andrew going to get the shirt online?

3. Why is Andrew getting it online instead of at the store the next day?

Answers

1. He wants a certain shirt in a size large.

2. He's going to get it online because they only have small and medium sizes in the store

3. He wants to get it delivered to his house.

At the Movie Theater

Matt is buying some tickets for a movie.

Ticket Agent: Hi, what would you like to see?

Matt: Batman.

Ticket agent: Sure, the next **showing** is at 7:00. Is that good?

Matt: Yes, please.

Ticket agent: For how many people?

Matt: Four.

Ticket agent: Okay, and any **preference** of where to sit?

Matt: Somewhere near the back please, in the middle. Oh, and my wife likes the **aisle seat.**

Ticket agent: Sure, we have some seats **available.**

Matt: I'd like to get some snack **combos.** Can I pay for that here?

Ticket agent: No, you can order that at the **concession.**

Matt: Sure.

Ticket agent: Okay, here are your tickets. You're in theater 6 at 7:00.

Vocabulary

Showing: Viewing, screening (usually of a movie).

Preference: Liking one thing instead of another thing.

Aisle seat: A seat that is not in the middle of a row.

Available: Free; not used.

Combos: Combinations.

Concession: A place where you can buy snacks or drinks at a sports event, movie theater, etc.

Practice

1. Where's the _____? I want to get a soda and some popcorn.

2. I have tickets for the 3:00 _____.

3. Would you prefer a window seat or an _____?

4. Let's check if they have some _____. It's probably cheaper.

5. Do you have a _____ for where we go for dinner?

6. Let's see if there are some seats still _____. It's kind of last-minute but you never know.

Answers

1. concession

2. showing

3. aisle seat

4. combos

5. preference

6. available

Terrible Hangover

Tom isn't feeling well because he had too much to drink.

Jenny: I'm bored! Let's go watch a movie.

Tom: Hey Jenny, I'm not feeling well right now.

Jenny: Oh no, what's wrong?

Tom: I know it's my fault but I have a terrible hangover.

Jenny: Why do you always drink so much? I hope you at least had a fun night. Do you need anything?

Tom: Could you grab me some aspirin, please?

Jenny: Sure, I'll pick you up a bottle and stop by.

Check your Understanding

1. Does Tom regularly drink too much?

2. What is Jenny going to bring Tom?

3. What does Jenny want to do?

Answers

1. Yes, he does.

2. She's going to bring him some aspirin.

3. She wants to go to a movie with Tom.

At the Library

Kevin wants to check some books out of the library.

Kevin: Excuse me, can I **check out** some books?

Clerk: Sure, have you got your **library card**?

Kevin: Oh no. I don't have an account. Can I **sign up**?

Clerk: Sure, do you live in Pitt Meadows?

Kevin: Yes.

Clerk: Can I please see your **driver's license**? I can get all the **info** I need from there.

Kevin: Sure.

Clerk: Okay, here's your new card. You can use the number to sign up for an account online. You can check out 10 books at a time for three weeks. You can **renew** them online **up to three times.**

Kevin: Great, thanks.

Vocabulary

Check out: Many different meanings but in this case, it means "to borrow."

Library card: Something that allows you to borrow library books or use other resources at the library.

Sign up: Join.

Driver's license: A card that allows you to drive a car legally.

Info: Information.

Renew: Many meanings but in this case, it means to borrow the books for an additional 3 weeks.

Up to three times: Maximum of 3 times.

Practice

1. You can be late _____ at my job. After that, you get in big trouble!

2. I don't have my _____ with me. Can you look up my information?

3. I lost my _____ and have to make an appointment to get a new one.

4. Please _____ online. We don't do it at the desk here.

5. You can _____ only 3 DVDs at a time.

6. Please _____ online if you want to join the class.

7. Do you need more _____, or will that work?

Answers

1. up to three times

2. library card

3. driver's license

4. renew

5. check out

6. sign up

7. info

Opening a Bank Account

Lucy wants to open up a bank account.

Clerk: How can I help you?

Lucy: Hi, I'd like to open up a bank account, please.

Clerk: Sure, checking or savings?

Lucy: Oh, what's the difference?

Clerk: A checking account is an everyday account that you use to pay bills or make transactions. A savings account has a slightly higher interest rate and is for saving money, n(everyday use.

Lucy: I see. Okay. I need a checking account, please.

Clerk: Sure, can I see two pieces of ID?

Lucy: Yes, here you go.

Clerk: Okay, that's fine. I'll get it all set up. It'll just be a few minutes.

Check your Understanding

1. What kind of account does Lucy want to open?
2. Did Lucy know the difference between a checking and a savings account?
3. How many pieces of ID do you need to open an account?

Answers

1. She wants to open a checking account.
2. No, she didn't.
3. You need two pieces.

Ordering Pizza

Todd is ordering a pizza on the phone.

Employee: Hi, ABC Pizza.

Todd: Hi, I'd like to get a large pepperoni pizza, please.

Employee: Anything else?

Todd: No, that's it I think.

Employee: Sure, for pick-up or delivery?

Todd: Oh...umm...how much is delivery?

Employee: It's $5 if you live within a 10-minute drive. $10 for 11-20 minutes.

Todd: I see. Okay. I'll pick it up. How long until it'll be ready?

Employee: Give us 30 minutes. What's your name and phone number?

Todd: Todd and 123-456-7890.

Check your Understanding

1. Is Todd going to get his pizza delivered?
2. How long until the pizza is ready?
3. Does Todd want anything else besides pizza?

Answers

1. No, he isn't.
2. It will take 30 minutes.
3. No, he doesn't.

My Fridge is Broken

Tom is having problems with his fridge.

Tom: Hi, I'm having some problems with my fridge. Do you repair them?

Repair person: Yes, we do. What seems to be the problem?

Tom: It's not as cold as it used to be.

Repair person: How old is it?

Tom: Around 15 years I think.

Repair person: And what brand?

Tom: Samsung.

Repair person: Okay, we can send someone over. Is tomorrow okay for you?

Tom: Sure. Can you come in the afternoon?

Repair person: Yes, we'll be there at 1:00.

Check your Understanding

1. What's the problem with the fridge?

2. Is someone going to come fix it?

3. How old is the fridge?

Answers

1. It's not that cold.

2. Yes, someone will come to fix it tomorrow.

3. It's 15 years old.

Gluten-Free?

Helen is asking about gluten-free options at a restaurant.

Waiter: What would you like to order?

Helen: I'm **gluten-free** and I'm wondering what **options** you have?

Waiter: There are a few things you might want to **consider**. You can get a gluten-free **bun** with any burger or gluten-free bread for any sandwich. We also have gluten-free pasta or gluten-free **pizza dough**.

Helen: Nice. Lots of things! I think I'll have the **veggie** lover's pizza with gluten-free dough, please.

Waiter: Sure, there will be a $3 **surcharge** for that. Is that okay?

Helen: No problem.

Waiter: Okay, great.

Vocabulary

Gluten-free: Describes someone who doesn't eat things with gluten (a wheat protein) in them.

Options: Choices.

Consider: Think about.

Bun: A round piece of bread that's often used for burgers.

Pizza dough: What pizza crust is made from. Dough is not cooked yet.

Veggie: Vegetable.

Surcharge: Extra fee.

Practice

1. Is there a _____ for that? How much?

2. There are so many _____ for ice cream flavours! I don't know what to pick.

3. Can you pick up some hotdog _____ on your way home?

4. I will have the _____ burger, please.

5. I'm thinking about going _____ this year and seeing if it helps my stomach issues.

6. Would you _____ switching to Thursday?

7. I made some _____. We just have to let it rise for an hour.

Answers

1. surcharge

2. options

3. bun

4. veggie

5. gluten-free

6. consider

7. pizza dough

Where's the Bathroom?

Larry is at the dentist's office and he needs to use the bathroom.

Larry: Hi, I'm Larry Smith. I have an appointment at 12:30.

Receptionist: Sure, have a seat, please. It'll just be a few minutes.

Larry: Do you have a bathroom here? I'd like to go before my appointment.

Receptionist: Sure, you'll need this key. It's down the hall and on your left.

Larry: Thank you.

Receptionist: No problem.

Check your Understanding

1. What time is Larry's appointment?
2. Is the dentist ready for Larry when he arrives?
3. Where is the bathroom?

Answers

1. It's at 12:30.
2. No, he is supposed to sit down and wait for a few minutes.
3. It's down the hall and on the left.

Where's my Package?

Sarah is trying to find a missing package.

Sarah: Hi, it says that my package was delivered this afternoon but I don't see it. I got a text message saying that.

Delivery driver: Let me check. What's your tracking number?

Sarah: 103239082.

Delivery driver: Okay. It wasn't delivered to your house because you weren't home. You can find it at the post office down the street but only after 6:00. Do you see a delivery notice paper in your mailbox?

Sarah: Oh. There it is. I got it. Thanks for your help.

Delivery driver: Sure. You can pick it up today after 6:00.

Check Your Understanding

1. Why is Sarah calling?

2. Where is the package now?

3. Where can Sarah get her package after 6:00?

Answers

1. She's calling because she wants to know where her package is.

2. The package is probably on the delivery truck now. It will be at the post office at 6:00.

3. She can get the package at the post office.

Before You Go

If you found this book useful, please leave a review wherever you bought it. It will help other English learners, like yourself find this resource.

You might also be interested in this book: Advanced English Conversation Dialogues. You can find it wherever you like to buy books. It has hundreds of helpful English idioms and expressions. Learn to speak more fluently in American English.

Made in the USA
Las Vegas, NV
01 November 2023

80040414R00046